DEDICATION

With love to my father,
Euclid Israel Rabior,
a man of prayer

D0109402

CONTENTS

■ ■ ■

PSALM 71

In you, O LORD, I take refuge;
let me never be put to shame.
In your righteousness deliver me and
    rescue me;
incline your ear to me and save me.
Be to me a rock of refuge,
a strong fortress, to save me,
for you are my rock and my fortress.

Rescue me, O my God, from the hand of
    the wicked,
from the grasp of the unjust and cruel.
For you, O Lord, are my hope,
my trust, O LORD, from my youth.
Upon you I have leaned from my birth;
it was you who took me from my
    mother's womb.
My praise is continually of you.

I have been like a portent to many,
but you are my strong refuge.
My mouth is filled with your praise,
and with your glory all day long.
Do not cast me off in the time of old age;
do not forsake me when my strength is
    spent.

For my enemies speak concerning me,
and those who watch for my life consult
    together.
They say, "Pursue and seize that person
whom God has forsaken
for there is no one to deliver."

O God, do not be far from me;
O my God, make haste to help me!
Let my accusers be put to shame and
    consumed;
let those who seek to hurt me
be covered with scorn and disgrace.
But I will hope continually,
and I will praise you yet more and more.
My mouth will tell of your righteous
    acts,
of your deeds of salvation all day long,
though their number is past my knowl-
    edge.
I will come praising the mighty deeds of
    the Lord GOD,
I will praise your righteousness, yours
    alone.

O God, from my youth you have taught
    me,
and I still proclaim your wondrous deeds.
So even to old age and gray hairs,

O God, do not forsake me,
until I have proclaimed your might to
    all the generations to come.
Your power and your righteousness, O God,
reach the high heavens.

You who have done great things,
O God, who is like you?
You who have made me see many
    troubles and calamities,
will revive me again;
from the depths of the earth
you will bring me up again.
You will increase my honor,
and comfort me once again.

I will also praise you with the harp
for your faithfulness, O my God;
I will sing praises to you with the lyre,
O Holy One of Israel.
My lips will shout for joy
when I sing praises to you;
my soul also, which you have rescued.
All day long my tongue will talk of your
    righteous help,
for those who tried to do me harm
have been put to shame, and disgraced.

PRAYER OF BLESSING FOR THE PRAY-ER

May the living God touch you through
these prayers, and in turn, may you
touch God.
May God's healing hand restore you.
May God's saving grace strengthen you.
May God's quiet voice guide you.
May God's loving arms embrace you.
May God's angels watch over you.
May God's tender mercies give you
peace.
May your friends bring you comfort.
May your family bring you joy.
May your faith bring you hope.
May the kindness and compassion you
show to others come back to you a
thousand times over.
By giving, may you receive all that your
heart desires, and by loving, may you
be loved lavishly in return.
With all my heart, I bless you, in the
name of the Father, and of the Son,
and of the Holy Spirit.
Amen

GOLDEN AGE, GOLDEN OPPORTUNITIES

For you, O Lord, are my hope,
*my trust, O L*ORD*, from my youth.*

PSALM 71:5

❖ ❖ ❖

I'M PROUD OF WHO I AM!

Good God,

I'm so very proud of who I am! I may not be young anymore, but I am still a worthwhile, good person with tremendous value.

I am your beloved child, and nothing is going to change that. My body may be aging, but my mind, heart, and soul are young, and I'm still excited about being alive.

I never want to stare at life from a distance. Instead, I need to be active and involved. I want to live my life to the fullest. I want to continue to blossom and bloom, learn and live—and bring all the love and goodness into this world that I possibly can.

Yes, I'm older now, but in many ways, that makes me even more valuable to you. These golden years into which I have entered provide golden opportunities for so many things I still can do for you.

God, I'm alive with pride! I really do have so much to offer, so many things to contribute, so much life experience to draw upon in helping others. I am able to serve you more effectively than I ever have before.

Show me daily, then, how to do just that—to serve you by serving others, even in the smallest ways—through a smile, by taking time to listen, through a simple act of encouragement, or by offering a prayer for someone's needs.

Thank you, dear God, for bringing me to this point in my life. I'm glad to be where I am. I'm glad to be alive. Above all, I'm glad that I belong to you now and forever.

All that I am thanks and praises you for all that I am and will yet become with the help of your grace.

Amen

THERE IS LIFE AFTER RETIREMENT!

Lord,

People often say that when retirement comes, the end is near—and besides—without a job what is there to live for?

Well, I am living proof that that's a bunch of nonsense! There is life after retirement. Just look at me!

In many ways, my life is richer, happier, and busier than before I retired. The difference is now I'm doing what I want to do, when I want to do it, and how I want to do it.

I'm my own person now, and I love who I am! My body power may have diminished somewhat, but I have more soul power than ever before. I feel like a young person: enthusiastic and alive!

Aging is not just something physical; it is also an attitude. I intend to keep my attitude positive, hopeful, and happy as long as I live.

Thank you for this special time of my life, Lord. These days are precious, and these are truly golden years, filled with the sunshine of a meaningful, good life—helping you by helping others.

Yes, there is life after retirement. Thanks, Lord, for proving that through me!

Amen

PRAYERS
FOR MY FAMILY

O God, do not forsake me,
until I proclaim your might
to all the generations to come.

PSALM 71:18

❖ ❖ ❖

PRAYER FOR MY FAMILY

Lord Jesus,

Families are never perfect, and mine, like every family, has plenty of flaws and imperfections. Yet, I love my family dearly and want only the best for each of us.

That's why I am asking you to richly bless my family, Lord. Bond us closer together in love and shape us into a happier, healthier, holier family—more like the one you experienced at Nazareth.

And if there is any repair work I personally need to do when it comes to mending relationships, help me do it so that I can bring healing to my family. If I have hurt or damaged relationships, may I lay aside my foolish pride and ask forgiveness so that reconciliation can take place. If I am the one who has distanced myself from family members, help me bridge the gap between us and reunite. If I have damaged family communication, show me how to improve it.

I am willing to do whatever is necessary to increase love, peace, and understanding in my family, and I ask your help to achieve these wonderful goals.

Thank you, Lord, for this family of mine. They are one of my greatest gifts, and I truly love them with all my heart. Bless us well, Lord, and save each of my family members so that we all can take part in the great family reunion you have promised to those who belong to the kingdom of God.

Amen

PRAYER FOR MY SPOUSE

Lord,

What a joy it is to grow older with my best friend, my partner in life, my spouse. I know that our marriage has not been perfect, but for the most part it has been wonderful, and that's enough for me.

We have loved, fought, and dreamed together, and now we find ourselves facing old age together. More than ever, I am grateful for my spouse's companionship.

In your providence and plan for our lives, you brought us together, and for this I thank you. And even as you blessed the wedding feast at Cana and replenished the wine for the newly married couple, replenish the wine of our marriage. Help us make the time remaining for us rich and exciting, filled to overflowing with love.

Show us how to grow together, build together, and bond even more closely into soul mates.

Thank you, Lord Jesus, for the gift of our marriage. May you continue to be our companion until the two of us join you in the great, joyous wedding feast in heaven.

Amen

FOR A FAMILY MEMBER WHO HAS LEFT THE CHURCH

Lord Jesus,

(N.) has chosen to leave the Church and no longer practice the faith. This decision has left me disappointed and hurt. It is a decision that I am having a difficult time respecting—and yet I know I must.

And although it may be hard, I will not lecture or scold (N.) for that decision, nor will I nag or interfere in any way. I can, however, bring my feelings to you in and through this prayer.

I ask you to touch (N.) through the power of your Spirit. May he (she) rediscover the joy of sharing faith with a believing community. (N.) may not agree or even care, but we need him (her) very much. We, as the body of Christ, are poorer and weaker without him (her).

Lord, if we have wronged or hurt (N.) in any way, show us how to bring about healing and reconciliation so the home-coming is made easier.

In the meantime, I place (N.) in your hands. You want what is best for him (her), just as I do. I trust that you will speak to his (her) mind and heart, and I pray that your voice will be heard.

Amen

PRAYER FOR
MY GRANDCHILDREN

God, thank you for my grandchildren.

If I have to put into words just how much I love them, I would say that it's all the way up to the heavens and back again. May my love for them reach out to hug and embrace them all through this prayer.

Lavish your richest blessings upon my grandchildren, God. Protect and guide them down whatever roads of life they choose. Make them strong enough to bend—but not break—when the storms come, as they surely will.

And in all the circumstances of their lives—both the joys and the sorrows— may they know you as their God and as their best friend, just as I have known you for so many years. I know that you love them infinitely more than I do. May your saving grace bring them and each of my family members to the glory of your reign, where we will be reunited forever.

Amen

PRAYER
FOR MY CHILDREN

Gracious God,

Years ago you gave me the gift of my children, and now I do not want a day to go by without thanking you for this priceless gift.

Not a perfect gift—that's true. They have disappointed me, let me down, and hurt me deeply at times, but that has nothing to do with my love for them. Just as you love me unconditionally in spite of all the ways I've failed you, so I have tried my best to love my children in the same way. My love for them, like their love for me, has not been perfect. In fact, there were times when it was inadequate and badly flawed, but nevertheless, it has always been genuine, true, and unceasing.

I want to give my children the kind of love that comforts and supports, encourages and affirms; I want to love them into the best persons they can become. I never want my love to suffocate, control, or overwhelm them, but instead, to give them freedom, peace, and permission— if they need it—for new growth.

Above all, I don't want my children to wonder if I love them. Help me make it clear to them at every opportunity that I have truly loved them more than life itself.

I place them in your hands, dear God. Bless and protect them, touch their minds with your wisdom, walk with them down their life paths. Be their shepherd and Lord, just as you have been mine. Take care of them. And one glorious day, bring all of us together in a joyful family reunion in your reign.

They are my children, God, but they are also yours. And your love for them is infinitely greater than mine. Together, as we blend your love and mine, may they be touched, healed, and empowered to become the persons you have created them to be.

For the wondrous gift of my children, God, thank you now and forever.

Amen

WHEN I LOOK BACK ON LIFE

I still proclaim your wondrous deeds.

PSALM 71:17

THINGS I LEARNED
ALONG THE WAY

Lord,

When I ran away from you, you came after me and invited me back home.

When I ignored you and stopped talking to you, you continued to speak to me.

When I was angry at you and even when I hated you, you still loved me and cared for me.

When I despaired and wanted to die, you gave me hope and encouraged me to go on living.

When I fell and could not go on by myself, you lifted me up and carried me.

When I sinned, you forgave and forgot.

When I lost my way, you came and found me.

When I devalued myself, you clothed me with dignity and affirmed me as your beloved child.

When I yielded to darkness of mind and soul and took myself far too seriously, you set me free and taught me how to laugh again.

When I doubted you, you stood by me and believed in me.

When I thought I was unlovable and not worth saving, you saved me.

When I was wounded and aching in mind, heart, and spirit, you healed and restored me.

Never for a moment have you abandoned or forsaken me. How much you must love me!

Thank you, God.

Amen

IF I HAD MY LIFE TO LIVE OVER

Creator God,

If I had my life to live over, I would definitely do some things differently. I would care more and criticize less. I would give more of myself and my resources without being so concerned about what I would get in return.

I would talk less and listen more. I would complain less and praise more. I would laugh more, instead of frowning, scowling, and yielding to gloom. I would trust more and fear less.

I would take better care of the earth. I would take better care of myself as a temple of the Holy Spirit. I would slow myself down and smell more flowers. I would open my eyes and ears to the beauty all around me. I would tell people how much I love them. I would heal more and harm less. I would spend much less time trying to change others and work harder on trying to change myself.

For the gift of my life, God, I thank and praise you. But if I had it to do over, with your help, I would change some things. I would make my life better for myself and others. I would be a better instrument in your service.

Amen

THANKS FOR
THE MEMORIES

Gracious God,

My memories are so very important and precious—more valuable than any jewel that I have ever owned. There are so many of them now, and they dart into my consciousness when I least expect them. I may look at a photograph, hear a song, view a Christmas scene, or watch a child learning to walk, and it's as though a switch were thrown, and my mind lights up with a recollection from the past.

Not all of the memories are good, of course, but most of them are. And now, even the painful ones seem muffled and dull.

I remember so many persons and events with tenderness, and with deep gratitude and joy. What a gift these memories are! How wonderful it is to be able to remember and relive some of my past.

You have your memories, too, don't you, God? In your living Word, you tell us that you will remember us always— that you have carved our names in the palms of your hands. When everyone else on this earth has forgotten us, you remember.

How could you forget us? You have made us for yourself, and you have loved us with an everlasting love.

Thanks for the memories, God—all of them. And thanks for remembering us both here and in eternity, where we will see you face to face and be with you forever.

Amen

VOICES

Lord,

There have been so many voices in my life. There are voices from the past, of people now long gone. There are voices from the present, of family, friends, and strangers. There are even familiar voices from radio and television of people I don't know, but whose voices I have learned to recognize.

Of all the many voices in my life, the one voice I want to hear most is yours. Help me, Lord Jesus, to hear you as you speak to me. As you call me by name, I want to respond. I want to go wherever you take me.

Open my ears that I may hear your voice this day.

Amen

PRAYERS
OF GRATITUDE

My mouth is filled with your praise.

PSALM 71:8

❖ ❖ ❖

LITANY
OF THANKSGIVING

For the gift of time, all that is behind me
and all that remains before me—
thank you, Lord.

For my family and friends, those living
and those deceased—
thank you, Lord.

For all the love I receive from you and
from so many others—
thank you, Lord.

For all the love I am privileged to give in
return—
thank you, Lord.

For the gift of laughter and all the happi-
ness I have known—
thank you, Lord.

For the trials and sorrows I have experienced, which matured me and taught
me compassion for others—
thank you, Lord.

For the talents and special gifts you have
given me and for the opportunities to

put them to good use—
thank you, Lord.

For all the glories of nature that mirror
your goodness and beauty—
thank you, Lord.

For those you send to me when I need
them—
thank you, Lord.

For sending me to those who need me—
thank you, Lord.

For the joy of prayer—
thank you, Lord.

For the gift of my body, and all the plea-
sure it has allowed me to experience—
thank you, Lord.

For the gift of faith, which has given me
eyes to see you and ears to hear you—
thank you, Lord.

For the healings I have experienced and
was able to bring to others—
thank you, Lord.

For the crises I have survived and the
obstacles I have overcome with
your help—
thank you, Lord.

For those who believe in me and help
me believe in myself—
thank you, Lord.

For all those who affirm and encourage
me when I want to give up—
thank you, Lord.

For those who have paved the way for
me and made the present possible—
thank you, Lord.

For the times I have received mercy,
understanding, and forgiveness
instead of shame, guilt, and punish-
ment—
thank you, Lord.

For my life and my story and the
positive ways my life has impacted
others—
thank you, Lord.

For your promise of eternal life—
thank you, Lord.

For all the uncountable blessings I have
received, the ones I know about and
the ones I will know about only when
I see you face to face—
thank you, Lord.

From the depths of my being—
thank you, Lord.

Amen

THANKSGIVING FOR AN ANSWER TO PRAYER

Benevolent God,

Thank you for hearing and answering my prayer. At moments like this, your love for me and your kindness toward me are so overwhelming that words cannot fully express my gratitude to you. Yet, because you read my heart so well, you know how grateful I truly am for this answer to my request.

All good gifts come from you including the answer to this prayer. So I praise you for your great goodness and give thanks to you with all my being.

Amen

PRAYERS
FOR SPECIAL PERSONS

My mouth will tell of your righteous acts.

PSALM 71:15

PRAYER
FOR A DEAR FRIEND

Lord,

Thank you for my dear friend (N.). She (he) is special to me beyond words. My life has been so greatly enriched by this friendship, that when I think of (N.) my heart is filled to overflowing with gratitude to you for sending her (him) into my life. Bless her (him) richly this day, and help me recognize opportunities to be a loving friend in return.

Thank you, Lord, for your friendship and goodness to me too, all the days of my life. You have loved me with an everlasting love. You have called me by name, and I am yours forever.

May the love I show to my friends and to all others reflect your great love which led you to lay down your life for your friends.

I thank you and praise you, now and forever.

Amen

PRAYER
FOR MY PASTOR

Lord Jesus,

I ask you to bless and take care of
(N.), my pastor. Being a pastor has never
been easy, but in today's Church, with
all the demands and expectations placed
upon our spiritual leaders, it's more
difficult than ever before.

May (N.) be supported by personal
faith and nurtured by our love. May (N.)
enjoy health in mind, body, and spirit,
and be continually renewed in your love.
Give (N.) the courage to preach the gospel
without compromise, and with the loving
compassion that makes the gospel mes-
sage real. Give my pastor the wisdom that
can only come from your Holy Spirit, your
Spirit that guides us all to eternal life.

Lord, our pastor is responsible for us,
but we are also responsible for our pastor. May we work together, and never
fail to lift up (N.) in prayer, with support, affirmation, and encouragement.

Amen

PRAYER FOR MY DOCTOR

Lord Jesus, Divine Physician,

May your Holy Spirit guide and direct my doctor today. Stand by his (her) side, especially as he (she) makes decisions which may affect lives for years to come. Give him (her) the strength to endure the overwhelming demands of this profession, and may your compassionate love flow forth to his (her) patients through him (her).

Show him (her) how to not just treat hurting bodies but to minister to the whole person so that the mind and spirit are treated as well.

Bless my doctor, Lord. Like you, may he (she) bring healing and hope to all the suffering who come to him (her) this day.

Amen

DAILY PRAYERS

You will increase my honor,
and comfort me.

<small>PSALM</small> 71:21

MORNING PRAYER

Kind God,

I thank you for this new day, full of promise and purpose—a gift from your hands. I am ready to face whatever this day brings, confident of your presence and power at work in my life.

Help me to live for you today, God. Remind me of what I can be for you.

Open my eyes to the wonders this new day brings. Help me to see the many opportunities to serve you by helping others.

I commend this new day into your hands and ask you to bless it with love and life. Especially bless all those who will touch my life in the hours that lie ahead.

I'm ready, God. Let's move into this brand-new day together and transform it into something beautiful for you and me both.

Amen

EVENING PRAYER

Lord,

Thank you for seeing me through this day—another day closer to returning to you. Bless the work that my hands and heart accomplished this day. Even in the smallest ways, may it further your plan and purpose for our world and your kingdom present in it.

Bless all of the persons I encountered today. They have their own unique joys and sorrows, and I hope that by what I said and did, I was able to minister to them, ease their burdens, and light their way.

Forgive me any failings and sins committed this day, either deliberately or by omission. Above all, forgive me for not loving with your love, for not forgiving with your forgiveness, for not reaching out the way you would. Forgive me if I did not allow you to work in and through me today.

Always, Lord Jesus, I ask you to forgive my sins and remember me in your kingdom.

Now, I commend both my soul and body into your hands. Grant me a restful sleep and a quiet night, and bring me to a new day ready to serve you. Even in sleep, Lord, I belong to you. Both in waking and in sleeping, may I find comfort and peace in your abiding presence with me.

Amen

GRACE BEFORE A MEAL

Gracious God,

Thank you for all the many ways that you nourish me, especially through my family, friends, and friendship with you.

Bless those who have no food this day—those who are hungry, homeless, and helpless. Bless the whole world, so badly in need of your healing love.

For all the blessings I have received from you throughout my life, I thank you from my heart.

Bless this food now. May it strengthen me so that I may serve you by serving others with greater love, generosity, and compassion.

Amen

PRAYERS FOR MYSELF

You are my strong refuge.

PSALM 71:7

❧ ❧ ❧

PRAYER FOR COURAGE

Lord Jesus,

These may be my golden years, yet getting older is not easy. It demands versatility to face shadows as well as sunlight, valleys as well as peaks, and many losses in spite of all the gains that come from living a long time. In particular, it demands courage.

Grant me, then, the gift of courage to face all that life has brought me and is yet to bring. May I see life as a challenge, not an intrusion or, worse yet, a curse.

Help me not to succumb to fear, anxiety, and worry, but to trust that you who have guided me this far in my life's journey will see me through to the end and beyond.

I ask for the courage not to become hard, cynical, or uncaring, but in fact, to be more loving, more compassionate, more forgiving, and more concerned than ever before.

What I want is the courage to be more like you in every area of my life, and to be eager to let others see how you are living in and through me. More and more, may I find the courage not to run from life, but to embrace it, bless it, and share it generously with others.

Help me find the courage to take the time that remains for me and transform it into something positive and good—something productive and rich for me and for all those who touch my life. Fill me with courage and show me how to encourage others, so that their lives are made better, happier, and more fulfilling by the special strength you alone give and can give to others through me.

Amen

PRAYER FOR
MY FINANCES

Bountiful God,

Living on a fixed income isn't easy. Since retirement, managing my money has often been a struggle that leaves me upset and anxious.

When I start to feel this way, I need to anchor myself in you. If you can take care of the lilies of the field, you can certainly take care of me and my limited finances.

I would like to have more money, not just for my own needs but to help those who are less fortunate. Even though I may not have much, I recognize my obligation to share my resources as best I can with those in need.

I do believe that by giving, I myself will receive, and that you will prosper me in ways that will surprise and delight me.

Thank you, God, for all that I have. Show me daily how to use it wisely and well.

Amen

PRAYER FOR GUIDANCE

God of Wisdom,

I am your child, and with the trusting faith of a child, I come to you now with this special concern which is uppermost in my mind.

(Mention your need.)

Lord, I seek your guidance and direction in this matter.

May the Holy Spirit enlighten me so that I may not only make a good decision but also a decision that is in accord with your will and plan for my life.

Lead me, as only you can. Show me what to do in this matter, as only you can. Give me wisdom, as only you can.

I pray with an expectant faith that you have heard this prayer and will give me the guidance and discernment I seek. I seal this prayer in the name of Jesus, the Lord and Light of our world.

Amen

PRAYERS
OF FORGIVENESS

*Do not forsake me
when my strength is spent.*

PSALM 71:9

LITANY OF FORGIVENESS

For the times I lacked compassion and
concern for others—
forgive me, Lord.

For my failures to pray and take the time
to talk to you—
forgive me, Lord.

For not sharing my resources: my time,
talent, and treasure—
forgive me, Lord.

For holding grudges and refusing to have
a forgiving heart—
forgive me, Lord.

For the times I have criticized
and gossiped—
forgive me, Lord.

For not reaching out to comfort and
console others—
forgive me, Lord.

For putting possessions ahead
of people—
forgive me, Lord.

For not caring for myself physically,
    emotionally, and spiritually—
    forgive me, Lord.

For ignoring the needs of my family
    and friends—
    forgive me, Lord.

For excessive consumerism and
    materialism—
    forgive me, Lord.

For the ways I misused nature and
    damaged the environment—
    forgive me, Lord.

For closing my mind to new ideas
    and opportunities—
    forgive me, Lord.

For talking more than I listened—
    forgive me, Lord.

For my prejudices, biases, and deliberate
    acts of discrimination—
    forgive me, Lord.

For being greedy—
    forgive me, Lord.

For deliberately tuning you out and
ignoring your guidance—
forgive me, Lord.

For the misuse and abuse of the wonderful gift of sexuality—
forgive me, Lord.

For failing to see your face in the homeless and the helpless—
forgive me, Lord.

For believing I could save myself—
forgive me, Lord.

For not living fully for you—
forgive me, Lord.

For my lack of faith, hope, and love—
forgive me, Lord.

For doubting that you can and will forgive me unconditionally—
forgive me, Lord.

For doubting that you love me with an
everlasting love—
forgive me, Lord.

Amen

I FORGIVE

Merciful God,

Your living word tells us that you not only forgive our offenses, you forget them. I have a hard time with both. Forgetting past hurts and those who have hurt me is almost impossible. I have never been, nor ever want to be, an amnesiac.

But I do want to be able, more and more, to forgive those who have hurt me, wronged me, disappointed me, failed me, and even damaged me. I want to forgive them, because I too have hurt many in the course of my life—and I want to be forgiven even as I forgive. The two really do go hand in hand.

God, I also know that forgiveness is a choice, a decision. It is not an emotion. I may not feel forgiving at all, yet in and through this prayer, I choose to forgive, especially the following person(s):

(Name them.)

I may have to pray this prayer over and over, because the old attitudes and grudges do not go away easily.

Help me too, God, to forgive myself for real or imagined failures. Show me how to let go of the past, to stop beating up on myself, so I can eliminate my self-hatred as I grow in self-love.

This prayer represents my decision to be and become a more forgiving person—toward others and toward myself—so that I may experience healing, peace, and renewal through this change.

Amen

HEALING PRAYERS

You will bring me up again.

PSALM 71:20

❤ ❤ ❤

HELP ME TO BE GENTLE WITH MYSELF

Loving God,

So many times when I look back at my life, I focus on my failures and inadequacies—all the things I didn't do and should have done, and the many things I didn't do well. I am my own worst critic, and often I am far more critical than kind.

Of course, my life has not been perfect. Yes, I did make mistakes, I failed, and I sinned. But none of that makes me a failure. You still love me unconditionally, and I want to love myself that way too. Teach me to be gentle with myself.

My flaws do not make me a loser. I am a winner, precisely because I am made in your image and likeness—and even with my flaws, that will never change. Besides, there is nothing you cannot forgive. You have forgiven my worst sins and set me free.

In being gentle with myself, I want to be set free from the harsh, judgmental attitudes I so often manifest toward myself. I want to learn to be as kind and gentle toward myself as you have been to me. I believe that with your help, I can learn to relate to myself in this way.

For your gentleness and for the gracious love, mercy, and compassion you show to me daily, dear God, I thank you with all my heart.

Amen

PRAYER FOR PEACE

God of Perfect Peace,

I pray for peace in our troubled world, in our country, in the Church, in my family, and in my own life. In all that I say and do, may I truly be a genuine instrument of your compassion and peace. Even in the smallest ways, show me how to bring the healing power of your peace to those I touch this day.

Teach me how to be a peacemaker in every circumstance of my life. By knowing your peace in my own heart, may I help bring it to the hearts of others.

Let there be peace on earth, and let it begin with me.

Amen

PRAYERS ON
SPECIAL DAYS

*It was you who took me
from my mother's womb.*

PSALM 71:6

♥ ♥ ♥

PRAYER ON MY BIRTHDAY

Gracious, Loving God,

How good it is to celebrate this day, when you first loved me into life. How good it is to be here on this earth and to enjoy its splendor and wonder. How good to be a member of the human family!

You have woven my days together into the unique tapestry called "my life." Even though it has not always been easy, it has always been good, and I am grateful.

May I remember, Lord, that all the days of my life have, in some way, been your steady gift to me. I celebrate that gift today, Lord, with gratitude and hope. I look forward to tomorrow and the next day and the next, trusting in your presence and grace.

For all my years, I thank you, even as I thank you for this new year ahead and dedicate it to you.

Amen

PRAYER IN
TIMES OF SICKNESS

Compassionate Friend,

I don't feel well at all today. My body, mind, and spirit all seem to be ailing.

Praying is particularly difficult when I hurt, but I bring this simple prayer to you to ask for your help—for myself and for all those who are suffering in any way in our world. May I not yield to discouragement or despair, but hold tightly to your hand and walk with you during this difficult time.

I ask for your healing touch upon all of us—upon all who will experience pain of any kind this day. We are all in need of your mercy, compassion, and love.

In some way, may I, and those I have prayed for, experience you this day working in our lives for our recovery and well-being.

Thank you, gracious God.

Amen

THE PHONE DOESN'T RING MUCH ANYMORE

Lord,

The phone doesn't ring much anymore. My family is all grown up and gone, many of my friends are gone too—and I miss them all. I miss the hustle and bustle and all the activity of the past—but the quiet phone doesn't mean that my life is over.

Direct and guide me to new areas of growth and service. If I'm not getting many phone calls, maybe I need to phone others who can benefit greatly by hearing from me. They may be shut-ins, sick persons, or just people who are discouraged and disheartened. I can call them and offer a word of encouragement and hope. By phone, I can keep company with those in need.

Lord, I know that the telephone can be a powerful instrument in your service. I can use it to communicate love, care, and concern for persons in need. I can touch the lives of others without even seeing their faces, especially by listening to them from the heart.

A kind, interested voice over the phone can be an important means of helping and even healing someone else. It can be a genuine blessing for me and for those you send me to, even if only through a telephone call.

Use me as only you can, Lord. Use all of my resources, such as the telephone, in your service. May your Holy Spirit inspire me to say just the right thing at just the right time. Let my voice become your voice as I share your love with others in need.

Amen

LORD, I FEEL LONELY

Lord Jesus,

Right now I'm feeling lonely—lonely to the very core of my being. I want to be wanted, needed, and loved by somebody, but instead, I feel isolated and alone.

I suppose I'm feeling sorry for myself, but this loneliness is almost like physical pain. It actually hurts, and hurts badly. The feelings of loneliness also feed my depression, and then I end up on the edge of despair.

You are no stranger to loneliness, Lord. In the Garden of Gethsemane, you were nearly crushed by the same pain I'm feeling. Like me, your heart broke with grief, sorrow, and the feeling that no one cared about you. You know what I'm going through.

I don't like these feelings, Lord. They are too dark, too controlling. They make me lose my perspective so that I think far too much about me and too little about others.

Call me forth, Lord Jesus, from this tomb of loneliness. Call me to new life, just as you did with Lazarus. Help me leave these dead feelings behind and move into the sunshine of your love.

With you as my Lord, I can never really be alone. You are only a prayer away. And besides, there are others just as lonely as I am. Send me to them, and them to me, so that together we may experience healing.

Thank you for your friendship, Lord, and for saving me not just in eternity, but right here, right now, today. Thank you, Lord Jesus, for helping me work through these lonely feelings to emotions of peace.

Amen

PRAYER BEFORE SURGERY

Lord Jesus,

I pray for your healing touch upon my body through the surgery about to take place. Guide the hands of the doctor and all who assist in the surgery. Use their skills to restore me to health and wholeness.

I ask you to remove any fear or anxiety from my mind, and fill me with the peace which you alone can give. I place myself completely in your hands, Lord Jesus, trusting in your care and love for me. May my recovery be swift, my strength renewed, and my health restored, so that I may serve you even more effectively.

Bless those, Lord, who are concerned about me today. I appreciate their love and support, and ask you to be with them in a special way. Remove all fear and anxiety from their minds as well.

For your healing presence, thank you, Lord.

Amen

IT'S BEEN SUCH
A WONDERFUL DAY!

Good God,

It's been such a wonderful day—a pleasant day in every way. Everything has gone smoothly, and I feel peaceful and joyous in my mind and spirit. Nothing really unusual has happened, but I just feel great, and it's good to be alive and about.

Thank you for all my days, but especially for a day like this that has a special sweetness I will not soon forget.

I praise you, God, from whom all blessings flow, including the blessing of this marvelous day, which comes from you as gift.

Amen

ETERNAL LIFE

Incline your ear to me and save me.

PSALM 71:2

❦ ❦ ❦

WHEN I THINK ABOUT DYING

Lord Jesus,

When I think about dying, I get frightened. Yet, I know what I believe. I believe that when I die, my life will be changed, but not ended. After all, an end is always a beginning. At the horizon, earth becomes sky. Where the sand stops, the magnificent ocean begins. And when this life as I know it ceases, eternity begins.

The sun may seem to set on my life, but it never really does. Because you are the Resurrection and the Life, I have the greatest confidence, born of faith, that I will be with you forever.

Because you are the Good Shepherd, I believe that you will walk with me through the dark valley of death to green pastures and new life. With you at my side, it will be a safe journey.

Because I belong to you, Lord Jesus, you will never abandon or forsake me. I believe—I know—that in my living and dying I can place my life completely in your hands with full trust and confident hope; you will not leave me disappointed. I will be safe with you always in the fullness of your kingdom. Nothing can ever separate me from your love because both in life and in death I am your servant and you are my Lord. With you, my soul will rejoice forever.

Amen

REST IN PEACE

Eternal God,

You are the God of the living, not the dead, and all are alive in you. Your Word tells us that love is as strong as death, but I believe in an even greater truth. I believe that love is stronger than death.

I still love the dear ones who walked with me for a time here on this earth and are now with you. I still carry them in my heart. And I believe that from where they are in eternity, they, in turn, reach out to me with love.

Love is the great golden thread that continues to connect us. It can never be broken or destroyed, for love is the only thing that endures. Love is forever.

I bless the memory of all those who have gone ahead of me marked with the sign of faith. I know you are a merciful God, and I trust in your compassion for them as well as for me. With you, they are safe. I commend them into your hands, even as I commend myself into your hands, now and always.

Until I see them again, may they rest in peace and find eternal joy in your loving presence.

Amen

PRAYER FOR SOMEONE WHO IS DYING

Lord Jesus,

(N.) is dying. Ease her (his) suffering and support her (him) with your strong, loving arms. More than ever before, may (N.) know you as her (his) Good Shepherd who will walk with her (him) through the dark valley of death to newness of life.

I pray, too, for her (his) family. Grant them the consolation of your peace, and may their faith be stronger than their grief.

Into your hands, Lord Jesus, I commend (N.). May she (he) pass through the gates of death in safety to the joys of eternal life with you forever.

Amen

HELP ME
HELP OTHERS

O God, do not be far from me.

PSALM 71:12

HELP ME
HELP SOMEONE TODAY

Lord Jesus,

Help me help someone today. It doesn't have to be in any big way—small is just fine. I know I can't solve everyone's problems or change the painful circumstances of their lives. But I can offer a word of encouragement, a smile, a hug. I can promise a prayer, and then keep that promise.

There are many forms of help I can give, if only I am attentive and aware, if only I notice needs and make some kind of loving response as best I can.

Today, may I be a Simon of Cyrene, lifting a heavy burden from someone's life, even if only for a few moments.

Use me.

Send me.

Show me, Lord Jesus, how to help someone today in your name.

Amen

SHOW ME HOW TO GET INVOLVED

God,

Now that I'm retired, show me how to get involved. I'm convinced that some retirees die of boredom and loneliness, and I don't want that to happen to me. May your Holy Spirit direct me to the people who need me.

There are so many things I can do for others. I can read, so that means I can help others learn to read. I have skills, so I can show others how to acquire these same skills. I can volunteer. I can befriend. I can make myself available to those who need me and my care and talents.

I want and need to be active. I would much rather burn out than rust out. I want my life to make a difference. I want to give myself away for your sake and for the sake of others.

People are waiting, God. Show me how to get involved, then send me. I'm ready, willing, and able, and I'll follow wherever you lead. My time is yours, and I'm ready to be used by you. Use me today, God—use me well.

Amen

MY HANDS

Lord,

The story of my life is written on my hands. These hands have done so much. Most of what they've done, I'm proud of; some, I'm not.

These hands dressed me in the morning, earned a living, changed diapers, held flowers and delicate crystal, wrote letters, and turned the pages of a thousand books and newspapers. They touched, embraced, stroked, soothed, and caressed. They waved hello and good-bye, rubbed tears away, and shook hundreds of other hands. And, yes, sometimes they were instruments of my anger. I regret those times I used them to hit, slap, punch, and strike.

Over the years, I have folded them in prayer and raised them in praise of you. And even now as I look at them, older and somewhat worn, I feel myself overflowing with gratitude to you.

So many times you blessed the work of my hands and used them to bring your love to others. In the time I have left in this world, take my hands, Lord, and make them your hands. Let those I touch know that they have been touched by you as well.

May my hands give generously, bless lovingly, and soothe compassionately. May they be your healing hands to ease the pain of others. I give you my hands, Lord Jesus. Use them as you please in your service.

Amen

SPECIAL INTENTIONS

But I will hope continually.

PSALM 71:14

PRAYER FOR MY FAITH COMMUNITY

Lord Jesus,

Pour out your blessings upon my faith community. May it truly be a Christ-like neighborhood—radiating your love, compassion, and forgiveness to both the local community and the larger world community. May we who make it up become more and more service-minded, and truly be persons for others, just as you yourself were the great man for others.

Keep us from stagnation, pride, and narrow-mindedness. May our doors always be open and our welcoming hands extended to the poor, the misunderstood, those discriminated against, and those who are often overlooked or ignored. May all who worship in our church and with our faith community experience your presence through the love, compassion, generosity, and hospitality of its members. May our church never become just another sacred building, but a living, dynamic body of love—

your body—so that those who have seen us, have seen you and know beyond a doubt that you are alive in us.

Make your light shine more clearly in and through our faith community, Lord Jesus. We belong to you. May our faith community believe that, and live that out by all we say and do.

Amen

PRAYER FOR OUR WORLD

Gracious God,

The old song says you've got the whole world in your hands. Please don't drop us. We are battered and bruised enough already, much in need of your amazing grace and saving love.

Is there any chance you could come among us and give us the help we need? But you've already done that, haven't you? You so loved our world, that you sent your own dear, beloved Son to bring us light and life.

You've done a lot, God, and you can't do it all. We too have responsibilities for our world. Your work on Earth must truly become our own if we are to know the healing and wholeness we long for so much.

Bless our world, God. Until we come to that new world with you, it's all we have.

Love us into life. Forgive us when we don't know what we are doing. Keep saving us until we are saved forever.

And lead us through the darkness we ourselves have created to the dawn of a new and better day—where faith triumphs over fear, love over hate, and goodness over evil—made possible, if only we truly live as your daughters and sons.

Amen